ANY KIND OF EXCUSE

Wick Poetry Chapbook Series Three
Maggie Anderson, Editor

Any Kind of Excuse
Nin Andrews

Orphics
Leonard Kress

Just One of Those Things
Sarah Perrier

The Several World
Will Toedtman

ANY KIND OF EXCUSE

Nin Andrews

The Kent State University Press

Kent & London

Library of Congress Catalog Card Number 2002069429
ISBN 0-87338-757-0
Manufactured in the United States of America

06 05 04 03   5 4 3 2 1

The Wick Poetry Chapbook Series is sponsored by the Stan and Tom Wick
Poetry Program and the Department of English at Kent State University.

Library of Congress Cataloging-in-Publication Data
Andrews, Nin.
    Any kind of excuse / Nin Andrews.
        p.   cm.—(Wick poetry chapbook ; ser. 3, no. 1)
    ISBN 0-87338-757-0 (pbk.: alk paper) ∞
    I. Title.   II. Series.

PS3551.N444 A86 2003
811'.6—dc21   2002069429

British Library Cataloging-in-Publication data are available.

This book is dedicated to all the Jimmys I have ever known.

CONTENTS

ACKNOWLEDGMENTS

I would like to thank the editors of the following journals in which the poems first appeared: *Black Warrior Review:* "Sundays"; *Cream City:* "Man-thing," "Sleeping Beauty"; *Double Room:* "What the Dead See"; *Green Mountain Review:* "Gills"; *The Journal:* "Being Mean"; *Ploughshares:* "The Dying," "The Right Kind"; *The Best of the Prose Poem:* "The Summer My Sister Turned Fourteen,"; *The Prose Poem:* "The Day Auntie Lou Saw God"; *Sudden Stories, a Mammoth Anthology of Miniscule Fiction:* "Miracles."

I would also like to thank John Lane for his friendship, encouragement, and inspiration. And Maggie Anderson for her selection and careful reading of the text.

WHAT THE DEAD SEE

after Frank Stanford

Back then I never let on. Besides, no one was there to set the record
straight, the womb we fell from, soused with liquor. And there was
any kind of excuse. I was younger than I ever knew, in air swim-
ming with insects. Sometimes, talking with the Baptist preacher
on the patio about the folks who have gone from this world, I felt
them, like they were fish bones caught in my throat. *The dead have
things,* he'd say, *they don't even let on to the devil they know. The
living does too.* Like my head was a transistor radio, he wanted to
find that gospel station, make me fear the Lord. His breath, warm
on my face, a whiff of fish thawing, the rain like small feet on the
lake. I'd watch it and sip from a green Coca-cola bottle slow, won-
dering what the Lord and devil don't know, seeing nobody seeing
us. Nights, when my folks came home late, the headlights crossed
my ceiling. Shadows kept falling and falling. I'd watch my sister's
boyfriend slip out. She was good at faking shit, like sleep, like car-
ing what she did. Afterwards, I'd listen. Sometimes the dark would
look at itself and sigh, and the wind would blow in the alfalfa field.
I'd hear someone whispering so soft, no one heard her words.

MIRACLES

It was Indian summer, after a change in weather brought the bees inside, when Grandma moved in. Jimmy, the farmhand, and I were sitting by the silo, waiting for the milk truck when she stepped out of a yellow cab, wearing a fur muff and a red satin cap. That afternoon when the sun burned through the mist, bees were crawling up the windows looking for holes in the screens. Before my mom could get a grip on her, Grandma had hosed every bug in our house down with Raid and taken over doing the laundry too. If there was a thing Grandma liked, it was clean clothes. And other things were dead bugs and the Lord, Jesus Christ. But she didn't want to be bothered with the clothes dryer. She liked our clothes hung outside, saying the Lord liked honest work, which meant something you did without a socket.

It rained so much that fall, all our lettuce got slugs and the wilt. My mom said the sheets mildewed. After my grandma took the linens in from the line, they were damp and crawling with daddy long legs. Mom would slip them in the dryer, whining under her breath about how Grandma had her ways of dipping into everybody's affairs like a pumpkin vine in compost.

Nights, while Grandma read me her favorite parts of the Bible, mostly about Jesus performing the miracles, I'd sweep my sheets with my fingers, feeling for bug legs. I never could figure how any insect could walk on those legs, thin and wispy as hairs.

CLEANLINESS IS NEXT TO GODLINESS,

Grandma always said. She never did
let a solitary hair slip out of place.
Most days she met me at the screen door
with a feather duster or our new Electrolux vacuum,
the hose sucking my blouse.
She said she liked her girls clean.
She said I was just coated
with dog hairs, horse hairs,
and God only knows what all else.
Fixing me like a flower bouquet,
tucking in my blouse, fluffing my bangs
or adjusting my barrettes,
she'd stare me down just to let me know
I was allowed in only if she said so.

AWFUL SWEET

Some nights I'd lie awake, listening
to the horses kick in their stalls and the soft meow
of summer nights, then sneak down the hall
on sock feet and slip into Grandma's bed,
try to grip the edge to keep from rolling into her.
She'd wake, dab me with honeysuckle perfume,
tell me how bad I smelled. I needed to bathe
myself once in a while if was going to keep
cozying up with heifers all my days.
Mornings, no matter how many times
I soaped those little spots she perfumed,
I never could get rid of that awful sweetness.

GILLS

By the time I was in third grade, I could swim three lengths of an Olympic pool underwater. I told my friends I had gills. I was fast, too, on account of the strange webbing that grew between my fingers. I liked to show it off, make sure everyone said: *That's really gross.* Gross was a first-class compliment.

I never let on I was getting holier by the minute. The minister always said, *We have a lot to learn from the dead. Let us follow the examples that have been set before us.* Like what? I asked. I figured one thing for sure: the dead never took any breaths. So I started practicing.

Sometimes I'd come home from school and brag. *I breathed only fourteen times.* Grandma would be busy doing something like whipping cream, and she'd just say *mmmhmm.* Of course I lost track, and maybe 14 was all I counted, but I had to be special at something. I never did want to be just ordinary. My favorite word was EXTRA-ordinary, with the extra in all caps. Just thinking about my powers, I felt like a superhero. I'd challenge anyone to a contest: *Bet I can hold my breath longer than you.*

That was before Tommy Maloney took me on. It was a Monday in March, and Tommy had a freshly buzzed head. He said his new dad made him cut it. Actually, it wasn't just buzzed; Tommy was bald. He had a new dad every year, and when we asked what his mom did, he said she didn't do anything. She just said *yes.* I tell you this because I want to explain. Tommy was strange. And I don't want to be blamed for what happened next. It was right in the middle of Mrs. Mullnex's spelling class when we started holding our noses. Mary Beth Wiley was playing referee. Pretty soon Tommy started to sweat. His head glowed like a red halo. I could have sworn it even smoked. For a moment, I thought he was going to explode. I was just about to say, *it's okay. You win.* Tommy fell over, slumped clear off the side off his chair, and spread out onto the linoleum. His head hit the floor and bounced, and his glasses broke; the lenses popped out of the frames. Mrs. Mullnex waved her hands and bobbed back and forth like a bowling pin that was hit but not knocked down. I was so bad, the principal said, did I know I needed saving from the Lord, *hisself?*

On the car ride home Grandma commented what I did wasn't exactly wrong. Sitting beside me, the wipers going slap-slap, the rain gushing off her black Buick, she suggested I might want to start breathing again. That the dead don't, as I always imagined, stay underground. Instead they float up like mist in spring. That's the way she pictured it, anyhow. *You can't keep a soul down,* she informed me, *no matter how bad things get.* That's when I let the air go, let it glide out and out. It felt so good, leaving, I could almost imagine myself ascending, rising along with it. Like the Lord, Mother Mary and all the heavenly hosts. I wondered if one day I'd levitate. Make everyone clap.

BEING MEAN

It was Grandma who'd catch me
putting sow bugs in a paper sack
alongside the cornpones and chicken thighs
my mother set aside for Jimmy's snack.
Pranks like that and my sassing folks
whipped her into such a state,
I could hear her in my dreams
alongside the Andalusian rooster
who crowed just about any hour of the night.

When I woke, she was already shaking
her dust mop out on the porch,
telling me a girl like me
best set her heart on the Lord
like a bee on a blossom
and wash my hands and change my trousers
more than once a week.

Sometimes she'd say just as sweet
as syrup, *It sure would be fine*
to have a fresh pot of coffee
with a lemon pecan muffin.
She and I would fix a little tea tray.

Sitting together on the glider,
she'd be gazing through me
as if she were seeing through glass
out beyond where the buzzsaw droned
and the wild roses bloomed, seeing
something she'd been wanting to forget
a long time. Her sweat dripped
onto the floor boards while she sipped
coffee and took up silence
and her whittling or sewing a buttonfly
on an old pair of jeans. I'd fiddle
with the stations on the transistor radio

and peel a dirty Bandaid off my legs so slow
I couldn't feel a thing.

If I asked what she was thinking
she'd say something short like:
There are some things, Child,
you'll be sorry you know.
Or: *You think you'll always*
be doing whatever you please?

Her words circling around me
like barn flies or those mean kids
on the playground I could outrun on days
I was quick enough to see them coming.

SNOW WHITE

White stone, lifted from the sandbar off the coast of Pawley's Island, surface, smooth as a geisha's skin. *What is it?* I ask, *a shoulder blade, a kneecap?* Always she turns her face away. Who can blame her, after sleeping for years in a glassy world, above her only green waves, sky, occasional gulls. *Did she hear them cry?*

Did she dream? Was she an insomniac, too? My grandma didn't know, or if she did, never said. She always did leave out the best parts of the fairy tales. *Don't you worry. Get your beauty rest now.* Outside my window the moon glowed. That was the year astronauts walked on it. Squinting, I wanted to see them take their first steps. To ask if God was with them in the dark, the God who made the gullies for the rain and the path of the thunderbolt and the moon. I didn't like Him. He bossed and ruled so much; I held my breath.

Hovering above my grandma's bed, a pale ghost, I fingered her vials of medicine, small white pills, her first loves, white as bone, white as her powdered skin. *Wake up, please, wake up.* She never moved when I felt for her breath, the pulse on the blue vein climbing her neck like a vine. Afraid, I curled up as close as I dared.

THE DAY GRANDMA LOU SAW GOD

It was a day like any other day.
I'd been down at the pond,
catching crawdads in a bucket,
watching a chicken hawk
circle overhead.
Grandma Lou was in the orchard
picking fruit.
For lunch my mother served cold biscuits
and stew.
Grandma Lou told us then she'd been out
gathering the pickling pears
when it happened.
The voice of God came through.
Lou, it said, *I'm calling home my faithful servant,
old Grandma Mason.*
She looked up at the naked air,
and saw the angels flocking like crows,
though to tell it honest,
she said, she could hardly see
for the light blazing.
Mark my words, Grandma Lou sighed,
forking out another heap of tomato beef stew.
Miz Mason won't be long for this world.

Dad kept chewing his food.
My mother picked a daddy-longlegs
off the magnolia blossom
and carried it outside.
No one paid Grandma much heed.
She always had a way
of forecasting doom,
knowing just who was dying
which week.
Said she could feel 'em
like a minnow
slipping between her palms.

A day or two after Miz Mason passed on,
Grandma Lou and I sat out on the porch
shucking corn and picking off earworms.
I asked her did she recollect
what the angels wore,
and if they played harps or dulcimers
like my mother did.
But Grandma Lou said it looked like
she wasn't one
to see God's minions up close,
but it must be gobs of them up there,
sort of like bees on the moon.

THE DYING

When Grandma Lou was dying
in the rope bed, no one said much.
I had pinworms, used to wake up
and hunt for them in the sheets.
Dad taught me rummy and chopsticks
on the piano. My mom took turns
with Sister May, wiping Grandma
down. Mostly I wasn't allowed in
but I peeked anyways, seeing how
she picked at her skin
trying to pull it loose.
Last thing she said was
she was going for a cool swim.
Dad pulled the curtains.
Sister May left the ball game on the radio
and went out to pull onion grass
in the cow pasture. She said
no one wants to taste death
and sour milk the same week.
In the night dogs woke me.
There were car lights in my window
and heat lightning.
I flicked on my light.
Mud daubers made nests
on the ceiling.
They were kind of humming.

BZZZZ

Dad watched me suck honey off my fingers,
lick the spoon and sink it back in the Mason jar.
Above me, dozens of flies clung to sticky paper
swinging beneath the ceiling fan. I stared at their wings,
thinner than tissue. She'd almost been a mother
to me, Dad said. No one could have predicted this.
What was I going to do without her to come home to?
I listened to the fan drone and asked,
did he know that girl flies have eyes spread apart
while all the boys are cross-eyed? Had he seen
that fly up on the corner window with white powder
like confectioner's sugar under its feet?
Grandma said flies like that caught diseases.
That's why they don't move. Look close
and you can almost see little granules.
But he just couldn't get over it. The other week
Grandma was fixing five zucchini pies.
She never would give her recipe to Cousin Ada.
Wasn't it was just like her, carrying secrets to the grave?
A fly buzzed above my plate, danced its legs
in my honey, then sped off in sharp-angled turns.
Dad stared out the window, past the towels flapping
on the line, almost as if he were expecting Grandma
to come strolling up the dirt path, red suitcase in hand,
the way she did that Saturday in Indian summer
when she announced, this time she was coming to stay.

THE SUMMER MY SISTER TURNED FOURTEEN,

July was so sweltering, the pond shriveled into a mud puddle, and polliwogs wriggled in the creek mud where cats swatted them out with their claws. Jimmy took up helping her in the vegetable garden, sinking in the tomato sticks and weeding the okra and beans and things. Nights he'd be waiting in the old tire swing. My sister would beg me to go out back with her and Jimmy while they'd sit side by side, the hairs on their arms almost touching, the two of them staring at ants crawling around a bucket rim or peeling labels off pop bottles while listening to the bullfrogs and katydids. Sometimes the rain smelled close as sweat, and heat lightning lit up the air where bats swooped. I'd get so bored, I'd say something silly to break the silence, but it seemed like sadness was always circling over us like a stranded angel or some kind of song I never could get the tune of, no matter how hard I listened or how long they waited.

THE NIGHT AFTER JIMMY SHOT THE RED FOX,

the whole house hummed like an electric wire;
the front door whined on its hinges,
so many coming and going.
I woke and sneaked down the steps,
curled into the couch by the wood stove,
expecting my dad to say:
What do you think you're doing out of bed?
He always was one to send me back
to where I came from.
Before he could say a word,
Jimmy stopped shooting pool
and came over to ask did I play tiddlywinks
or blow tunes on a coke bottle.
He closed his fingers over my naked knee,
and told how he scoped out the fox
I'd watched each dawn
just so I could see her, again,
slipping through the fog
lifting off the swamp,
her mouth full of chicken,
her ears rising above the weeds
like small flames or wings
before vanishing into the shadows
her life depended on.

HIRING THE ONE-ARMED MAN

or How Jimmy Came to the Farm

After being in the military, I've done my time.
Now I make my own rules, but I can work.
Yes Sir, I can work a farm with one arm
But I got this new one from the VA.
Let me show it to you.
Comes with its own attachments.
Insert a knife and fork or a screw driver.
if you want to.
Now, I ask,
who'd want to wrestle a man with silver on his hand?
I'm as good as a fighting cock with fittings on his legs.
I can really operate with this thing.
And all kinds of machinery, too.
That much they taught me overseas.
Mr. Shaver, they used to say,
he can fix anything.
And my son, Jimmy, he's a hard worker, too.
Doesn't do a lick in school
Can't hardly read his name.
But give that boy a pitchfork or a shovel,
and he'll sweat worth a man twice his age.
He likes to show off, too.
Sometimes I go for a smoke and come back.
Landsakes, Jimmy, I say.
Stop, why don't you? But he won't.
He says, Yes, Sir, No, Sir
and keeps right on shoveling.
So I teach him a thing or two.
Like how to fish and hunt groundhog.
Like how snakes smell in the July sunshine.
He can sniff good as a hound, that boy,
and tell when copperheads
are slipping around a haybarn.
I make sure I raise him right.

So he knows what he can't see.
Sort of like the arm I'm missing.
It's always hanging by my side.
When I reach out and touch folks with it,
I feel a body just like it is.
That way I always know who I'm dealing with.

THE DAY THE COWS GOT LOOSE,

my dad said he should have known better
than to hire some fella who all but said
he was done being told what to do.
No Sir, he liked to answer.
I don't care to.
But he was good at driving the tractor
and mending whatever broke.
Most days he stayed cool in the tool shed.
He lied a lot, said he'd done all kinds of work
he'd never begun.

One day he didn't come to work.
That night he sauntered to the barn, whistling.
Where you been all day? Dad asked.
*Down in the hollow, fixing the barbed wire fence
like you asked me to.*
Dad could smell the liquor on the air.
You closed the gate after yourself? My father asked.
Yes, Sir. I locked it up tight.
They watched the horses suck water from the trough.
You better be damn sure, Dad said.
Mr. Shaver just smiled,
Damn sure, he repeated. *You bet I am.*

5 a.m. the next morning, the phone rang.
Nobody heard it at first, ringing and ringing
with every fan in the house on high.
Ma'am? I heard the sheriff's voice.
*I hate to wake you,
but it looks like every heifer you folks own
is grazing on the freeway.*

All morning we spent rounding up cattle.
The neighbors helped, and Jimmy too.
But Mr. Shaver slept in.
Dad said he was too hung over to lift his head.

Every gate on the farm was swinging loose on its hinges.
Mr. Shaver swore he didn't know one thing about it.
After that, it was Jimmy who worked for us.
His daddy took sick and had to stay in the bed.
That's what Jimmy said.

SUNDAYS,

sitting beneath the fan in the kitchen,
the blade shadows going over
and over my face,
I listened to the gospel on the radio,
some Baptist preacher saying
it was high time
we learned to walk right
with the Lord. The sin
can leak from a soul
like oil from a rusty can.

Wasps crawled over and over
the bruised apples in the bowl
on the side table.
When the hymns began,
I picked burdock
from my knee socks and hummed along.
Bobby G., the hired kid from town
came up from the horse barn,
plucked a floating egg
from the jar of pickle juice
on the counter, the dirt
rising from his fingertips
in a dark cloud.

We never said a word.
Afterwards, I watched him head
down the dirt path to the stalls,
his body-glide inside his clothes
like some kind of music
was riding his skin.
I didn't let on
I was looking.
That's how much I liked him.

DANCE LESSONS

Sometimes, Jimmy said,
I don't know about you, Girl.
I really don't—all those classes
your folks make you take,
like dancing.
I seen how you move, too,
those long gowns
sliding across the floor,
like a fish, hooked and pulling wake,
then maybe jerking every once in while
from side to side.
Personally I don't care for it.
Me, I listen to String play banjo or guitar—
We call him String because he's skinny,
it's true, but also because he can pick a tune
on his strings any night
and set it loose in a person.
All you got to do then
is put your heels to the ground.
It's hard not to.

THE RIGHT KIND

There was this cock in our high school,
not that I had anything to do with it,
but we girls giggled about it
and wrote notes in class.
We said it had a job to do
and was often seen rising
behind its spandex suit
at the country club. It worked
pretty good, we figured,
but there was this one girl
who took up complaining about it,
like it was a meal that was too well done,
the service sloppy.
Too quick and not enough of it,
that was her joke
on Friday nights
when we drove through Mickey D's.
She'd punch out her pill and take it
with a swig of Coke, then talk
about who was in charge of it,
how it could be handled, and later,
when her back was turned,
we all whispered about her,
how she wasn't the right kind of girl,
and it wasn't the right kind of cock.

MAN-THING

I kept that man-thing for months until it grew thin as a sliver and green on the outside. I even let him rest on the windowsill, fed him sunlight, views and vitamins. Daily he sipped plant juices. On occasion I took him out for entertainment, showed him to friends. I could tell what they thought by their blank stares. After a while, his presence irked me. He made sucking noises when he slept. His breath smelled of a cabbage garden. Each day I could stand him less. Still, he offered himself up. When winter came, I left him out on the patio. The stem of the man froze to an icicle. I pulled him out like a splinter, and with a distant clinking sound, he shattered. Perhaps it hurt a little. I can't be certain.

PEARLS

I dreamt you kept a banjo
between your blue-jeaned legs

and you were liking singing off key.
One day you took me to the movies

just to slip your hands
up my skirt.

I went to the ladies room
and never came back.

That night the banjo played real loud
in my sleep.

You sent me two tiny strands of pearls
and some lame-brained excuse.

I wore those pearls around my thighs
for weeks, hoping

you had a clue how to set them loose.

STRANGE BIRDS

The year no one slept,
the rooster crowed just about any hour of the night.
He's one strange bird, Jimmy said.
Dad named him No Doze,
and when anyone asked what kind of bird he was,
my father said he was a Delusional.
Grandma thought he said Andalusian.
She was into pedigrees,
and she was sure No Doze was some exotic specimen.
All those overbred animals do peculiar things, she said.
I imagined No Doze coming by ship
from some place in another time zone.
Some nights I thought maybe weasels
were lurking around the coop.
Once I ran through the dark in my PJs
wanting to see.
But weasels are quick.
Footsteps sound like thunder
to snakes and weasels, Jimmy said.
Shoot, they can hear you roll over in the bed.
He said No Doze was just doing his job.
What more could we expect?
Besides, No Doze was a teenager
in a house full of hens.
Give him a few years, why don't you?
But the night Dad stayed up
waiting for Mazey, our mare, to foal,
he said No Doze just about drove him to the brink.
By the time the vet came, it was too late.
The foal had died in utero.
The vet just shook his head.
When birds act strange, he said, *it's always a bad sign.*
Grandma said she should have known.
She'd been suggesting for weeks
that someone was going to pass on.
She just couldn't say who.

Dad didn't believe a word of it,
but he turned No Doze loose, and all his hens.
The red fox picked him off in no time.
Jimmy said the rooster just fell over, toes to the sky.
Chickens do that.
Their hearts start beating so fast, they pass out cold.
That way they don't know when they're dead.
But we all heard it.
Silence like a farm at night with nobody crowing.
I stayed up late, listening.
Grandma said I best get used to it.
That's the way death sings.